DINOSAUR MYSTERIES

By Mary Elting and Ann Goodman

Illustrated by Susan Swan

Text copyright © 1980 by Mary Elting. Illustrations copyright
© 1980 by Susan Swan. All rights reserved. Printed in the
United States of America. Library of Congress Catalog
Number: 79-55035. ISBN: 0-448-47487-5 (Trade Edition);
ISBN: 0-448-13617-1 (Library Edition).
Published simultaneously in Canada.

Platt & Munk, Publishers/New York
A Division of Grosset & Dunlap

HOW TO PRONOUNCE DINOSAUR NAMES

All these names appear somewhere in the book. Here, in parentheses next to the regular spelling, each name has been divided into syllables and spelled somewhat like more familiar words. When a syllable is in capital letters, it is pronounced more strongly than the others.

Allosaurus (AL-oh-SAW-russ)
Ankylosaurus (AN-ky-lo-SAW-russ)
Archaeopteryx (ARK-ee-OP-ter-iks)
Brachiosaurus (BRAK-ee-oh-SAW-russ)
Brontosaurus (BRON-toe-SAW-russ)
Camarasaurus (KAM-are-ah-SAW-russ)
Camptosaurus (CAMP-toe-SAW-russ)
Ceratopsian (SARE-ah-TOP-see-an)
Chamosaurus (KAZ-mo-SAW-russ)
Coelurosaur (See-LURE-oh-SAW)
Deinocheirus (DIE-no-KY-russ)
Deinonychus (DIE-no-NIKE-us)
Dicraeosaurus (DIE-cray-oh-SAW-russ)
Diplodocus (Dip-LOD-oh-cuss)
Gorgosaurus (GAWR-go-SAW-russ)
Hadrosaurus (HAD-ro-SAW-russ)
Iguanodon (Ig-WAN-oh-don)
Lambeosaurus (LAM-bee-oh-SAW-russ)
Monoclonius (MON-oh-CLONE-ee-us)
Ouranosaurus (OO-ran-oh-SAW-russ)
Pachycephalosaurus
     (PAK-ee-SEFF-ah-lo-SAW-russ)

Protoceratops (Pro-toe-SARE-oh-tops)
Pteranodon (Te-RAN-oh-don)
Pterodactyl (TE-ro-DAK-till)
Pterosaur (TARE-oh-SAWR)
Rhamphorhynchus
     (Ram-foe-RING-cuss)
Saltopus (SALT-oh-puss)
Sauropod (SAWR-oh-pod)
Scelidosaurus (SELL-id-oh-SAW-russ)
Sordes Pilosus (SORE-des Pill-OH-sus)
Spinosaurus (SPY-no-SAW-russ)
Stegosaurus (STEG-ah-SAW-russ)
Struthiomimus (STROO-the-oh-MY-muss)
Styrocosaurus (STY-roe-ko-SAW-russ)
Supersaurus (SOOP-er-SAW-russ)
Syrmosaurus (SEER-mo-SAW-russ)
Tachycethalosaurus
     (TACK-ee-SEFF-ah-lo-SAW-russ)
Torosaurus (TAR-oh-SAW-russ)
Triceratops (Try-SARE-ah-tops)
Tyrannosaurus (Tee-RAN-oh-SAW-russ)
Ultrasaurus (Ultra-SAW-russ)

CONTENTS

ACKNOWLEDGMENTS

The authors and the artist gratefully acknowledge their debt to the many experts who have studied dinosaurs, written about them, put their skeletons together, and drawn their pictures. Recent work, especially by John H. Ostrom, Robert T. Bakker, and Adrian J. Desmond, has generated the new ideas about some of the wonderful creatures that appear in our book. We owe much to these three and to John C. McLoughlin who has written about dinosaurs and pictured them in original ways. Our warm thanks go to Vivian and Ed Jones of Delta, Colorado, for their generous guidance and help, and to Dr. James Jensen for a memorable evening after he had carefully lifted the shoulder bone of Ultrasaurus from the earth. Special thanks to Stephen Jay Gould who read our manuscript and made valuable corrections and suggestions. If errors remain, they are ours alone.

Mary Elting • Ann Goodman • Susan Swan

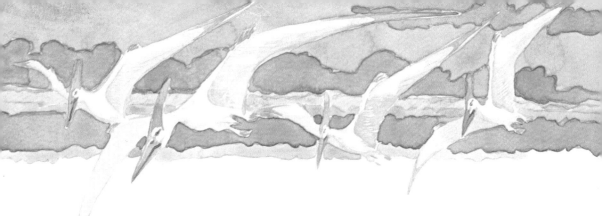

Giant Jaws and Terrible Claws   1

The gentle old dinosaur was just beginning its evening meal of twigs and leaves. It had strayed a short way from its companions and did not pick up the scent of a giant meat-eating dinosaur nearby.

Slowly, stealthily, the monster came closer. Walking on its hind legs, it stood almost as tall as the poplar trees in the forest. Its eyes glared beneath ridges of bone like the eyes of an eagle. In its vast open mouth stood rows of long, sharp, curving teeth.

Death was so sudden that the old plant-eating dinosaur never saw the four-foot long jaws that closed over the back of its neck, nearly cutting off its head. The curving teeth then ripped away enormous chunks of flesh that the killer swallowed whole. Because the great beast was so greedy and fierce, scientists named it Tyrannosaurus Rex, meaning "tyrant dinosaur king."

After its meal, Tyrannosaurus began to feel drowsy. It folded its hind legs, stretched out flat on the ground, and fell asleep.

Tyrannosaurus was one of the biggest of all meat-eating dinosaurs. It grew to be 40 or 50 feet long, and it weighed 16,000 pounds or more. With its heavy hind legs, big clawed toes and huge head, it looked like the scariest monster an artist could invent—except that it was *real*.

There is a mystery about Tyrannosaurus. Why did it have such puny arms? They were only 30 inches long, while the hind leg bones were as big around as a man, and more than twice a man's height. The arms ended in two claws that could not possibly have reached Tyrannosaurus's mouth—or even have touched its great overhanging jaws. Then what use could they have been?

Some scientists suggest that Tyrannosaurus did use its arms. Suppose it had been asleep after a huge meal, lying flat on its belly with its big head stretched out in front. When it got ready to stand up, it would have had a problem. If it gave a heave with its hind legs, it would just shove itself forward, scraping its chin in the dirt. But what if Tyrannosaurus first hooked its small fore-claws into the ground, then slid the hind legs under its body until it was sitting up like a chicken? Now perhaps it could straighten its legs and raise itself to full height with no trouble.

It would be impossible to find proof that the tyrant king had to get up in this awkward manner. Perhaps the real reason it had such puny arms is that they

didn't need to be any bigger. The huge dinosaur didn't have to grasp its prey. Like sharks today, Tyrannosaurus was a giant killing machine built around a pair of jaws.

Ages before Tyrannosaurus lived on the earth, there were similar meat-eaters. One called Allosaurus had a head that stretched! Both the jaws and the skull could spread apart at the center. This meant that the animal could widen its mouth for a colossal bite—an even bigger bite than Tyrannosaurus could manage.

A much smaller meat-eater lived about 50 million years before Tyrannosaurus, and it had a very different way of getting its nourishment. Its name was Deinonychus, meaning "terrible claw." And, indeed, its main weapons were claws, not jaws.

Deinonychus stood only five feet tall and weighed much, much less than Tyrannosaurus—only about 160 pounds. It had strong arms with skillful clawed hands for grasping prey, and it ran swiftly on the toes of its hind feet. Only two toes on each of these remarkable feet ever touched the ground. A short third toe ended in a sickle-shaped claw five inches long and terribly sharp. The claw was held upright when Deinonychus was running, so it didn't get chipped or dulled. Then it snapped down like a dagger to make the kill.

Scientists who discovered the skeleton were astonished to find that Deinonychus had a special kind of

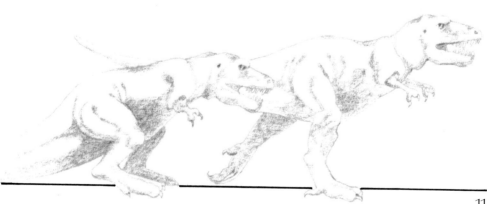

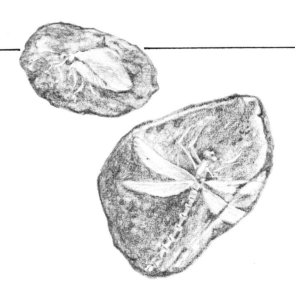

tail. It was equipped with very thick tendons that ran all the way along it on both sides. The tendons held the tail in position, straight out and stiff.

Why did such a nimble little creature need so stiff a tail? This puzzle was solved when scientists figured out how it killed its prey.

In order to use its deadly claw, Deinonychus had to perform a ticklish balancing act. First it attacked and managed to get a good grip with its hands. Then it had to stand on the toes of one hind foot while it raised the other foot and slashed down with the claw to tear open its victim. This would have been impossible if Deinonychus had had a floppy tail. But the stiff one

Deinonychus

gave the body all the balance it needed and kept it from toppling over. If these small monsters hunted in packs, they might have been bold enough to attack large animals.

Could anything be more scary than Tyrannosaurus and Deinonychus? Probably. An enormous meat-eater's hands and arms have been found in Asia. Each hand was as long as your whole arm, and each arm was as long as a big man is tall. Their owner could easily have grabbed another huge animal and ripped it to pieces. And what do you suppose scientists named this fierce new creature? Deinocheirus, meaning "terrible hand"!

2 Supersaurus and the Sauropod Mysteries

It is midsummer. The tall man's face and clothes are damp with sweat, and he is covered with white plaster dust. At his feet lies an odd-shaped block of plaster with a heavy iron chain wrapped around it. The block weighs several tons, yet the tall man acts as if it were as fragile as a teacup. He signals to a younger man at the controls of a truck with a winch on it. The crane on the truck rises, tightening the chain. Slowly, gently, the driver eases the great block into the bed of the truck.

The tall man relaxes. He has just lifted the bone of an unknown dinosaur—the biggest dinosaur ever discovered!

Safely coated with plaster to keep it from getting broken, the bone can now be taken away from the place where it had been lying for 140 million years. When the plaster is chipped off, scientists can study the bone, and museum visitors can marvel at its size.

This happened in August 1979, at a dinosaur dig in western Colorado. The site was Dry Mesa Quarry, sometimes called just "the bone hole." The tall man who dug up the huge bone is a scientist, nicknamed "Dinosaur Jim." His real name is James Jensen, and he has discovered more new kinds of dinosaur than any other person in North America. Bones from 12 of the new ones came from Dry Mesa Quarry. Many of them are being studied in Dr. Jensen's laboratory at Brigham Young University in Utah.

Of course, these aren't like the chicken or fish bones you leave on your plate after dinner. They have been lying buried in the earth for so long that they have mostly turned to stone. Such bones are called fossils.

Dr. Jensen began digging at the quarry in the summer of 1972. Some friends had seen a stony bone sticking out of the rock on Dry Mesa. Knowing that fossils should be removed only by experts, they telephoned Dr. Jensen, who came to investigate.

One of the first things he uncovered was the end of a very large shoulder bone. He could tell it had belonged to a plant-eating dinosaur, because it looked as if it had been full of little holes, like a sponge, when the animal was alive. The bones of meat-eaters are harder and seem to be made in layers. The farther Dr. Jensen dug around this shoulder bone, the more it amazed him. Completely uncovered, it was eight feet long. No plant-eater known at that time had a shoulder bone that big.

Soon Dr. Jensen found the dinosaur's neck bones. The largest measured five feet in length. This creature had a neck so long it could have looked over the roof of a four-story building. The tallest dinosaur ever discovered before could only have looked into third-story windows.

This had to be a new and super kind of dinosaur. Dr. Jensen nicknamed it Supersaurus.

Shoulder bone of Supersaurus

Who would have guessed that just seven years later, in 1979, Dr. Jensen would find an even bigger shoulder bone in Dry Mesa Quarry? This one was nine feet long, and it did not look like the Supersaurus bone. Its shape was different. That is how Dr. Jensen knew it did not just belong to an extra-big Supersaurus. It was a bone from an even larger creature—one of Supersaurus's relatives. Dr. Jensen called it Ultrasaurus. Ultrasaurus could have looked into the windows of a six-story house.

If you think that Supersaurus and Ultrasaurus do not sound like real dinosaur names, you're right. The scientist who discovers a new kind of animal gets to give it a name that will set it apart from all others. Often the name is a Greek or Latin word for something about the animal that is unusual. If it is a dinosaur, the name often ends with the Latin word *saurus,* meaning "lizard." For example, Brachiosaurus was the first dinosaur known to have front legs—that is, arms—that were longer than the back legs. Its name means "arm lizard."

Dr. Jensen says he does not yet know enough about Supersaurus and Ultrasaurus to give them their final scientific names. So for the time being, their nicknames will have to do.

What did Supersaurus and Ultrasaurus look like? Dr. Jensen believes they were members of a family of dinosaurs called sauropods, which means "lizard feet." Sauropods were huge plant-eaters that walked on all fours. They had rather small heads, long necks, and very heavy bodies. Some other dinosaurs in the sauropod family were Brachiosaurus, Brontosaurus and Di-

← *A sauropod herd*

plodocus. Supersaurus and Ultrasaurus looked most like long-armed Brachiosaurus.

For 150 years after the first sauropod bones were discovered, most scientists thought they knew how the animals lived. A sauropod, they said, must have been a sluggish creature that waded in lakes and swamps, eating water plants. Its great body seemed too heavy for legs alone to carry. So it was supposed to have stayed most of the time in the water, which buoyed it up as if it were an inner tube with legs. In the water, it would have been safe from attacks by the ferocious meat-eaters that lived on land. It would only leave the water long enough to lay eggs on the sandy shore.

Those were the old ideas about sauropods. Almost everyone believed them. But new ideas began to upset the old ones at about the time Dr. Jensen discovered Supersaurus. For example, a young scientist named Robert Bakker said he didn't think sauropods were swamp dwellers. Their toes were stumpy and short like elephant toes, and their big straight legs formed pillars strong enough to support their bodies. Sauropods, like elephants, seemed built to live on land. If a sauropod had been a wading animal, it would probably have resembled a hippopotamus, which has short legs and spreading toes. It would also have had a short neck like a hippo, because most water plants grow in shallow places.

Other scientists realized that sauropods would not have been safe from meat-eaters, even in the middle

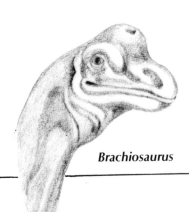

Brachiosaurus

of a deep swamp. Giant crocodiles would have been lurking there. Crocodile jaws six feet long could have snipped the slender sauropod necks in one crunch.

What use would sauropods have for such a long neck? Like giraffes, they could have reached up to eat leaves from the tops of trees. That would have suited them very well. Being so big, they needed to eat a lot, and they would have had the treetop food supply all to themselves.

A whole bunch of big dinosaurs that ate tons of plant food a day would quickly strip a forest bare. Soon, all would have to move on in search of more trees. Does this mean that sauropods traveled together in herds? There seems to be proof that they did. Thousands of fossil footprints have been discovered in rock, which millions of years ago was soft mud. In one place, the tracks show that 23 sauropods were moving together in the same direction. At another location, footprints of young dinosaurs appear in between two groups of larger tracks. Protected on both sides, the young ones would have been safe from meat-eaters. In fact, the herd itself would have been protection for all its members. Not even a big Gorgosaurus would have dared to attack a herd of towering sauropods. It would have waited for stragglers or for some animal easier to kill.

One mystery that has puzzled scientists for a long time is beginning to clear up. They know that some dinosaurs laid eggs. Whole nests of them have been discovered. But not even a scrap of fossil eggshell has been found along with sauropod bones. Why? Dr. Jen-

sen believes that young sauropods were probably born alive. Think how gigantic the egg of so large a creature would have to be. In order to hold the insides of such a huge egg together, the shell would have to be very thick. To break out of a shell that thick, Dr. Jensen says, a baby dinosaur would have needed a jackhammer.

People trusted the old ideas about sauropods for a long time. It took a great deal of studying and thinking to imagine that they were forest dwellers, moving about in groups. One person who found the new ideas hard to believe asked: "Wouldn't sauropods marching closely together have trampled on one another's long, dragging tails? Wouldn't there be lots of broken tail bones in quarries?"

This brings us to the mystery of the missing tails. It started with something puzzling about a group of fossil sauropod footprints in Texas. Prints of dragging tails should have been there, too. But they were not. Why?

Perhaps the tails did not drag after all. Some bone experts now believe that the sauropod was built rather like a bridge—the kind with tall towers and cables. Muscles, like bridge cables, could have held the tail up in the air.

Another mystery was the sauropods' dull peg-shaped teeth. How could they grind up tough plant food? Perhaps sauropods only nipped off leaves and

Brontosaurus

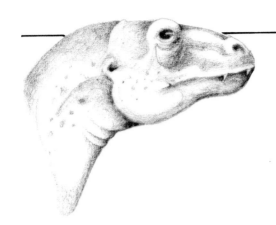

Allosaurus

twigs and swallowed them without chewing. Maybe the chewing was done in their innards. Some scientists believe that they must have had gizzards like present-day chickens. A gizzard is a kind of pouch with a rough, hard lining. Here tons of food could have been ground up with the help of pieces of rock that the dinosaurs swallowed. Smooth, rounded "bellystones," or gastroliths, are often found with dinosaur bones.

Supersaurus

These had once
been rough rocks
but were smoothed
down as they helped
the gizzards grind.
Perhaps sauropods had
several inside pouches, like
extra stomachs, that helped make
use of rough and not very nourishing
food. Cattle, deer, and some other
animals have special inner organs or
pockets in their intestines where bacteria
live. These bacteria aren't harmful germs.
They are the kind that can digest rough

plant foods better than the animal's own stomach juices can. Inside a sauropod, bacteria might have gotten their own food by digesting whatever the big animals swallowed. At the same time, the bacteria created left-over substances that the dinosaur could digest.

All these ideas help explain the sauropods' strange shapes. They were heaviest in the middle because they needed space for grinding and digesting tons of food. They needed to walk on all four feet in order to support their food-factory stomachs. Their heads had to be rather small and light so they could lift them to the tops of trees.

Scientists are still puzzled about sauropod hearts. How could they have pumped blood high enough to reach heads 60 or more feet above the earth? The pumps themselves must have been enormous and very well designed. Brachiosaurus's heart is thought to have weighed over 100 pounds. Ultrasaurus must have had an even bigger one.

Was Ultrasaurus the biggest dinosaur that ever lived? No one knows. Someday Dr. Jensen—or someone else—may dig up an even bigger creature.

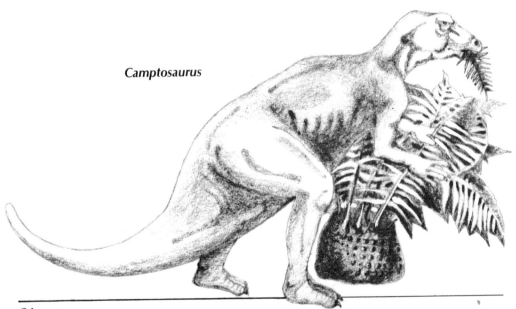

Camptosaurus

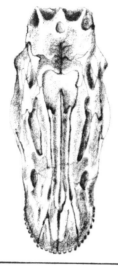
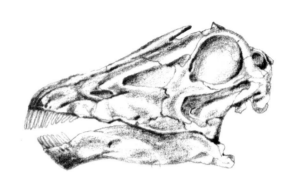

The Case of the Hole in the Head

Suppose you found a large neck bone in a dinosaur quarry. Then you found another and another. Finally, at the end of a neck 26 feet long, you found a skull. It wasn't like any skull you had ever seen. The teeth looked like fat, stubby pencils that hadn't been sharpened. Certainly not very good for chewing. Strangest of all, there were no openings in the skull where an animal's nostrils would usually be. Instead, this dinosaur had a hole in the top of its head.

"Why?" you would surely ask yourself. Why would a creature breathe through nostrils placed in this particular spot? That was one question scientists asked when they found the bones of the strange animal they named Diplodocus. They knew it was a sauropod, and at that time, many people believed that sauropods walked around in deep water. Could the hole in Diplodocus's head have been used for snorkeling? Walking with the top of its head above the surface, Diplodocus could have breathed through the hole.

Or so people thought.

Scientists have taken a new look at Diplodocus.

Many of them think the snorkeling picture is wrong. First of all, they say, Diplodocus could easily get around on land. Its bones were strong, but light. The neck bones, for example, had special hollowed-out shapes. They could support a lot of weight, just the way a three-legged stool will hold you up as well as a solid block of wood does. So Diplodocus did not need extra support for its body. In fact, said one scientist, its body was really so light it "would have floated like a cork in water."

But just supposing Diplodocus did manage somehow to walk on the bottom of a lake. It could not have breathed through the hole in its head.

Why didn't someone figure that out a long time ago? Probably the snorkeling idea was just too satisfying to give up. So dinosaur experts overlooked some important facts about breathing. These facts are the same for people and for other animals with lungs. When you breathe out, a kind of trapdoor at the top of your windpipe opens. At the same time, the muscles around your chest and lung area relax, and your breath is forced out. You can breathe out under water. So could a dinosaur. Actually, water presses against the body and helps to force air out. So far, so good.

But it's different when you breathe in. The trapdoor in your windpipe opens, and your breathing

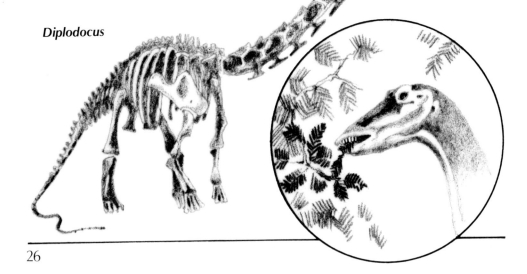

Diplodocus

muscles pull outward to make room for your chest to expand. Air then rushes in to fill your empty lungs.

Now think about Diplodocus with its lungs twenty feet down in the water. Water is heavy. Twenty feet beneath the surface there would be a great weight of water pushing down and around the animal's whole body. Breathing out, we know, would be easy. The weight of the water would force breath out like a gust of wind. But then, that same water pressure would keep the animal's chest from expanding. And so air could not rush in to fill its lungs. Even a dinosaur's mighty muscles couldn't work against the weight of so much water. In order to breathe in, Diplodocus would have to hustle out to a shallow spot.

That puts an end to the picture of Diplodocus the snorkeler.

In places where Diplodocus roamed, 130 million years ago, tall trees grew in great forests. With its long neck, it could have reached up and snipped off green stuff to eat. Its stumpy teeth were good enough for snipping. Then its gizzard and food-factory stomach would have done the rest of the work. So, it didn't need to wade around eating soft water plants.

Probably Diplodocus spent most of its time eating. This gives a clue to the location of the nostrils. High on the top of the head, they allowed Diplodocus to browse and breathe at the same time. Probably the nose was very sensitive to smells. When Diplodocus was looking for food, it could catch the odor of good things to eat. It could also smell any nearby enemy.

Diplodocus had a cousin named Dicraeosaurus, who was only 40 feet long. This smaller creature proba-bly ate plants that grew closer to the ground. It, too, had a hole for nostrils above the eyes. One artist

thinks that Dicraeosaurus may have breathed through a long nose, something like an elephant's trunk. If so, the picture shows how it might have looked.

Diplodocus was a close relative of huge, long-necked Brontosaurus and Brachiosaurus. They, too, had nostrils rather high on their heads, and for the same reasons.

Some scientists believe that all the members of this family may have liked to dunk and cool off in water sometimes, just as elephants do. If Diplodocus did spend some time dunking in shallow lakes or ponds, one scientist likes to think that it rested with its long neck floating straight out in the water. In that position, the hole in the head might have provided a handy way to breathe after all.

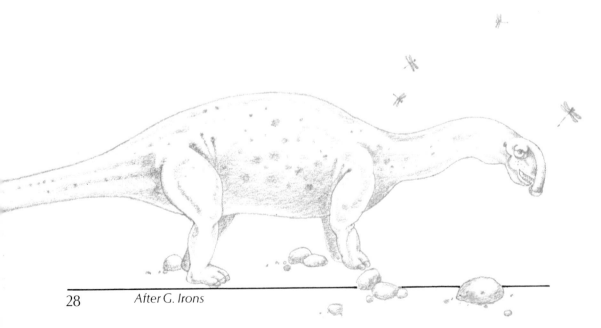

After G. Irons

4   What Did They Find in the Mummy's Stomach?

One day a dinosaur bone hunter found a giant skull that resembled a duck's skull. The wide, flat jaws really did look as if they could open and let out a tremendous quack. The animal that the skull belonged to was later named Hadrosaurus. That simply means "big lizard." But, before long, Hadrosaurus got a nickname—duckbill dinosaur.

Hadrosaurus, it turned out, was only one kind of duckbill. Half a dozen other kinds were soon discovered. They all had the long, shovel-like jaws. Some of their skulls were flat on top. But others had queer bony ridges or strange crests on their heads. Each of the new duckbills was given its own name, and the whole clan of cousins was called hadrosaurs.

People who studied the duckbills' skeletons thought that these dinosaurs must have behaved like ducks. Probably they paddled around in water, scooping up swamp plants with their beaks. There also seemed to be evidence that they had webbed toes like a duck's toes. Later, some scientists began to doubt this.

Some of the crests had hollow air passages inside. Did these tubes have something to do with breathing under water? Maybe the tubes were used for snorkeling. Or maybe they held extra air for duckbills to breathe while gobbling soft plants on a lake bottom.

By now you have probably guessed that these notions were wrong. First of all, like Diplodocus, who had a hole in the top of the head, a hadrosaur could not have snorkeled. The pressure of water on its chest would have kept it from breathing. And the nose tubes didn't hold enough air to be of real use, even for a quick, shallow dip in the water.

The shape of a hadrosaur jaw was certainly like a duck's bill. A duck has no teeth at all, and neither did the front part of the hadrosaur jaw. But the back part was quite different. It was loaded with an amazing set of grinders. There were five hundred or more teeth on each side, both upper and lower. More than two thousand altogether! Not only that. When any of the teeth got worn down or lost, new ones grew in. Would an animal that ate soft water plants be likely to have such teeth? Hardly.

Toes on hind feet ended in small hoofs. Would a water animal be likely to need hoofs? They would be more useful to a land animal that ran over hard ground.

The duckbills were beginning to seem less and less ducklike. But what did all the evidence really prove?

The best clue came from a mummy. A mummy is formed when a dead creature's body dries out before it has time to decay. That happened long ago when a hadrosaur died in a hot, sunny place. By good luck, no meat-eater came along to feed on the carcass. So the whole thing shriveled. The soft parts shrank, and the skin grew hard and leathery. Later, a flood washed the mummy downstream and covered it with mud. Finally,

After McLoughlin

31

the entire carcass became one big fossil. When it was dug up, the rock even showed the print of the skin.

Had any trace of hadrosaur insides been preserved? A scientist decided to cut into the rock where the mummy's stomach had been. And there he found what the duckbill ate for its last meal: pine needles, twigs, seeds. Not a sign of water plants. This was the fossil food of an animal that lived on land.

New knowledge has created a whole new duckbill story. Great herds of them roamed the ancient plains and valleys 75 million years ago. For the most part, they ran on swift hind legs, sometimes taking long leaps. The hoofs helped them to jump, to stop quickly, and to make fast turns. They could also put down their front feet if they wanted to browse on low plants. Their hard, strong bills were good for snipping and plucking leaves and twigs. Then the sharp teeth at the back of the mouth ground up the tough food so that it could be swallowed. Many plants contained a hard stuff called *silica*. Chewing on these plants wore teeth down very fast. So it was useful to have a supply of new ones waiting to grow out.

A few years ago a scientist found proof that rough food could damage dinosaur teeth very quickly indeed. He was examining a baby hadrosaur that had been discovered in Montana. There had been 15 small skeletons about three feet long, all lying together in a nest. These babies were too young to leave the nest permanently, yet their teeth were already worn from chewing on tough plants. The skull of an adult lay near the nest, probably the mother. She must have been guarding the babies when she and the little ones were killed together in some accident.

What about the mysterious bony crests? They still puzzle the scientists. Even if they had no other use, they certainly did protect the long nose tube that wound around inside. Probably the tubes were very sensitive to smells. Nobody knows, of course, whether a dangerous meat-eater did have a special odor. But if it did, the hadrosaurs could smell it approaching. The whole herd could then take off.

5 The Strange Case of the Great Horned Heads

What would you wonder about if you dug up some dinosaur skulls like the ones in the picture?

They all belong to a family called ceratopsians, which means "horn faces." The horns certainly are remarkable. So were the great bony plates at the backs of the skulls of these plant-eating dinosaurs.

What were they for?

Everybody agrees that the horns were for protection against meat-eaters. Each of the two sharp weapons above Triceratops's eyes was three feet long. The big horn on the nose of Monoclonius could poke into an enemy four feet away.

Ceratopsians did have to fight sometimes. How do we know? Skulls with broken horns give the clue. The broken bones mended, but scars from the breaks still show, even after millions of years.

Large, heavy bodies went with these skulls. Legs were strong and short. Roaming in great herds, the powerful beasts were among the last dinosaurs to live on earth.

What about the big sheets of bone at the back of the skulls? They look strangely fancy, and scientists began calling them "frills." At first, everyone thought a frill just helped to shield a ceratopsian's neck. Some meateater tooth marks have been found on frills.

Ceratopsian's own teeth may provide the clue to the bony frill puzzle. They, too, are amazing. Teeth in the upper and lower jaws slice past each other the way the two blades of a pair of scissors work. In one bite they could cut off a good-sized tree branch. Then all the tooth-scissors—several hundred of them—could cut the branch into bits small enough to be swallowed. To grab less woody food, such as palm leaves, a ceratopsian had a sharp, strong beak, something like a parrot's bill.

No animal could do all that chewing without strong muscles to move its jaws. Muscles always have to be anchored to bone. What bone? The frill! Sure enough, bone experts located the spots on frills where enormous muscles had been attached. So the bony shields could have been useful in at least two ways—for protection and to support muscles.

A great many questions about ceratopsians have been answered. But there is an important one that still causes arguments among scientists. Did the frill stick up into the air? Or did it lie back over the animal's neck, completely covered with skin? Pictures almost always show the frills raised and movable, like the drawing of Chasmosaurus on the left below. But John McLoughlin, who is a scientist and an artist, has a different idea. He thinks that muscles must have held the big plates of bone down tight. His picture of Torosaurus looks like the one on the right.

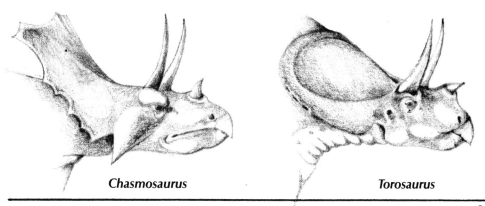

Chasmosaurus　　　　　　　　　　*Torosaurus*

Triceratops was about 25 feet long altogether, but it measured six feet from the tip of its beak to the back of the frill. That was about a quarter of its length. Penta-ceratops had an eight-foot head on a body 16 feet long. The prize goes to Torosaurus. Its head was nine feet long! And it had four-foot-long jaw muscles.

Young ceratopsians had be be protected until their horns grew long enough for self-defense. So they may

have huddled together, while the adults formed a circle around them, facing an attacker. Such a ring of terrible spikes could persuade even a whole pack of meat-eaters to look somewhere else for food.

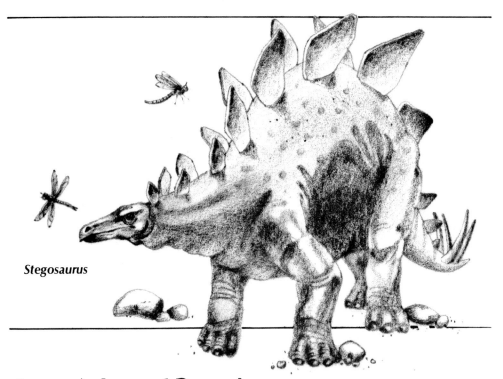

Stegosaurus

6 A Lot of Puzzles in One Skeleton

How do they put a dinosaur skeleton together? It's like doing the hardest kind of jigsaw puzzle. There are hundreds of jumbled-up parts, and it takes a lot of skill to figure out where they all go. Most baffling of all are the bones from a dinosaur that no one has ever seen before.

The first Stegosaurus bones ever discovered went together in a way that seemed all right—head, neck, legs, backbone, and tail. But then there were more than two dozen parts left over. Most of them were flat, leaf-shaped plates, some very large, some small. In addition, there were some sharp spikes, two feet long. None of these seemed to fit into the Stegosaurus skeleton. Where did the extras belong?

Only one answer seemed possible. Those bony plates and spikes must have been attached on the outside. Later discoveries showed that the plates had been arranged in two rows along the back, probably standing upright. Did they grow out from underneath the skin? Or were they hinged somehow to the skin's surface? These questions remained unanswered.

Next, what were the plates for? Were they meant to scare away enemies? Were they just for showing off, the way a peacock shows off its fancy tail? Or were they a kind of bony radiator that helped to control body heat? Perhaps blood circulated close to their surface. Air flowing over the skin would cool the animal the way a radiator cools a car. A scientist has actually tested this idea by putting a model of Stegosaurus in a wind tunnel. He found that the plates were arranged in the best way for catching a cooling breeze.

Another problem: Stegosaurus was about 25 feet long and weighed almost 8,000 pounds. But its head was tiny, and inside the skull there was room for a brain only a little bigger than a ping-pong ball. Its teeth were those of a peaceful plant-eater. Did it really have brains enough to outwit the meat-eaters that lived in its part of the world?

The tiny brain was just a small knob at the end of Stegosaurus's spinal cord. A spinal cord is a bundle of nerves inside the hollow backbone. Messages travel along those nerves from the brain to other parts of the body. But a strange thing turned up when someone studied Stegosaurus's backbone. There was space for a second knob toward the rear end of the spinal cord. Did Stegosaurus have two brains—one in front and one in back?

Not really. Most scientists think the enlarged space in the backbone may have been filled with a special

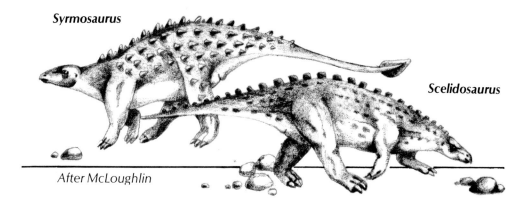

Syrmosaurus

Scelidosaurus

After McLoughlin

kind of gland. In case of danger, the gland could produce a substance that gave Stegosaurus quick energy for running or for defending itself. Ostriches have such a gland.

It hardly seems possible that Stegosaurus could outrun the nimble meat-eating dinosaurs. Its big, lumbering body was not built for speed. Its only defense equipment was its sharp spikes—four of them, each two feet long, attached to the skin at the end of its tail.

Stegosaurus is still a partly unsolved puzzle. Some scientists think that the bony plates were not radiators. They believe the plates gave protection against meat-eaters' teeth.

We don't know what Stegosaurus tasted like. Perhaps it just wasn't the meat-eaters' favorite food. That may be one of the reasons it managed to stay alive and to have descendants that survived for 50 million years.

The tiny Stegosaurus brain no longer seems as puzzling as it once did. Many other dinosaurs had brains that were small compared to their huge bodies. One expert says that these animals were not really stupid. Their brains were not too small. They were exactly the right size for the kind of body a dinosaur had, and also right for the life it lived. Another expert says that a brain is like a wallet. Its size doesn't matter—the important thing is what is in it. Dinosaurs certainly had enough in their heads to make them the most important animals in the whole world for 100 million years.

Other members of the armored dinosaur family were spiny and plated in different ways. Some of them looked like the picture on page 39.

Still other plated animals had even more wonderful armor. Ankylosaurus, for example, probably defeated almost any meat-eater, no matter how hungry it was. Its long, powerful tail ended in a vicious bony club. A blow from that heavy knob could break another animal's leg or knock out its teeth. About the only way to take a bite of Ankylosaurus would be to turn it over on its back. And with those spikes along its sides, that would not be easy.

Tachycethalosaurus

7 Mini-Mysteries

The Case of the Warty Bonehead

Some schoolchildren in Montana discovered an unusual dinosaur skull one day. Wart-like knobs stuck out of it here and there, and the top was dome-shaped. At first it seemed that this big, rounded head must have held a big brain. But no—the dome was solid bone! The new animal got the name Pachycephalosaurus, meaning "thick headed lizard." Most people just call it a bonehead.

Why should a dinosaur have bone nine inches thick on the top of its head? No one really knows. Such a thick skull might have given it protection from blows. Perhaps it had butting contests with other boneheads. That is what male bighorn sheep do today. The winner becomes boss of the flock.

What Did the Babies Eat?

We know what baby hadrosaurs ate. Their worn-down teeth show that they chewed rough, scratchy plants, just as their parents did. Those plants grew close to the ground, where little hadrosaurs could reach them.

Baby meat-eaters could chew on any animal their parents killed.

But what about a little Brontosaurus, whose long-necked parents fed on evergreen sprigs thirty or more feet up in the air?

The best answer seems to be that long-necked mother dinosaurs snipped off bits of food and gave them to babies. One scientist thinks the mothers may have fed their babies the way some birds feed their young. After food was partly digested in a mother Brontosaurus's own body, she could reverse the swallowing process. This would bring up a bit of mushy pulp, which she would drop into the baby's mouth. Pigeons feed their babies that way. So do doves and grouse.

The Case of the Missing Head

Have you wondered about the picture of Brontosaurus on page 21? It probably doesn't look quite like the Brontosaurus you are used to seeing. That is because scientists decided only in 1979 what kind of head the creature really had.

For some reason, the long-necked Brontosaurus skeletons were always found headless. Once, long ago, a few broken skull bones did turn up with a skeleton. But then, a complete skull was found nearby. It was the type of head that another long-necked dinosaur, Camarasaurus, was known to have had. Perhaps Brontosaurus, too, had this kind of head. After the bones were sent to a museum, this complete skull was put onto the Brontosaurus skeleton, and there it stayed.

Some dinosaur experts did have doubts about the head. The more they learned about Camarasaurus, the less they thought its type of head belonged on Brontosaurus. Finally, they got out those broken skull bones and looked at them again. By now, museum people had also learned more about all the long-necked dinosaurs. They could see that Brontosaurus was more like Diplodocus than like Camarasaurus. Sure enough, the

Camarasaurus

broken bones, when fitted together, resembled the skull bones of Diplodocus. A model was made in the museum, and now Brontosaurus in that museum has its own new head. It may soon have a new one in other museums, too.

The Case of the Tall Sails

Two unusual dinosaurs lived at the same time, about 75 million years ago, in Africa. Both looked as if their skeletons had two sets of ribs. One set hung down in the place where ribs always are. The other set of bones was also attached to the backbone, but it stuck straight up in the air. These spiny bones were covered with skin, making a kind of sail on the animals' backs. Some of the sails were as tall as six feet.

Were these sails a kind of radiator? Perhaps blood circulated through vessels close to the surface of the skin. Air blowing over the tall, thin spiny backs might

Spinosaurus

cool the animals on hot days. The one called Ourano-saurus was a plant-eater. Spinosaurus ate meat—probably Ouranosaurus meat.

The Case of the Poisoned Spike

In the days before people knew much about dino-saurs, a man named Waterhouse Hawkins made some models showing what he thought they looked like. Everyone supposed they crept around like lizards. So that was the way he built a huge model of the big plant-eater called Iguanodon. But there was one thing that puzzled him: A horn-like spike had been found with Iguanodon's bones. Where did it belong? About the only thing the spike seemed to resemble was a rhinoceros's horn. So Hawkins stuck it on top of Iguanodon's nose.

Such a marvelous creature, he decided, deserved a

Ouranosaurus

special celebration. He invited 21 people to dinner on New Year's Eve, and they all sat around a table set up in Iguanodon's belly.

At last, scientists found some complete Iguanodon skeletons. They could see that this animal did not creep like a lizard. Instead, it walked on its two hind feet. There was no place for a dinner table in its belly. And not one of the skeletons had a horn on its nose. Instead, a mean-looking spike stuck out from each of Iguanodon's thumbs!

To this day, no one really can tell how Iguanodon used the spikes. The best idea seems to be that they were weapons. If so, they were the only ones that the peaceful plant-eating creature had. Perhaps, if it was attacked, it could aim its spiked fists at the enemy's eyes. The thumbs don't seem big and sharp enough to rip very dangerous holes in a thick dinosaur hide. But could the spikes have contained poison— the way a snake's fangs hold venom? One scientist thinks that poisoned thumbs might have been a good form of protection. That is a mystery still to be solved.

Iguanodon

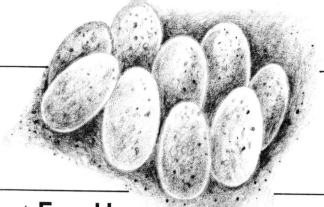

The Great Egg Hunt   8

An explosion was about to go off. Scientists looking for oil had prepared to blast near some rocky ledges in Montana. But before they blew anything up, they waited for some other scientists to get out of the way. This second group was hunting for dinosaur bones. They had almost decided to leave when one of them, a college student named Fran Tannenbaum, spied something. She let out a yell. What she had found was not a bone. It was a dinosaur egg.

The oil men postponed their plan to blast, and the egg hunt began. In the next few weeks, the hunters discovered nests that held 30 eggs altogether. Some had been broken before they hatched. A few were whole—the first whole ones ever found in North America. Not only that, they were the first meat-eating dinosaur eggs ever found anywhere in the world! The scientists knew that that was what they were because of something else they discovered. Near one nest lay the teeth and bones of a very small baby dinosaur that had just hatched. These were sharp, jagged meat-eater teeth. The bones were meat-eater bones.

Many plant-eater eggs have been found in other parts of the world. Some are almost round. Others have pointed ends, something like jelly beans. All of the newly discovered eggs in Montana were pointed. They measured 6 to 8 inches in length, and touching each other, they stood upright in the nests.

This arrangement in the nest is something that has always puzzled Dr. James Jensen. How could a mother dinosaur manage to lay a whole lot of eggs, all standing on their ends, none of them lying on their sides? Once Dr. Jensen made some model eggs and tried to

place them in that same neat arrangement. Impossible! One of them was always rolling over on its side before he could get the next one in position. He had to have someone help him set them all upright in the nest. Clearly, a mother dinosaur didn't just let the eggs drop into a nest any old way. She must have had an egg-laying organ of a special kind. What kind of organ it could be, Dr. Jensen hasn't figured out yet.

The first nests of plant-eater eggs delighted Dr. Roy Chapman Andrews in 1922. He and a group of other scientists had gone to look for fossils in the Gobi Desert in Asia. Until then, nobody was sure that dinosaurs really did lay eggs. On this trip, and on another trip three years later, Dr. Andrews and his associates found eggs of several different kinds in an area where there were many dinosaur bones. Some of the eggs were large, others quite small. They came in different shapes, too. Some lay on their sides, rather than upright, and they had been placed in neat circles, as if the mother walked around the nest as she laid them.

What kinds of animal had laid all these different eggs? Dr. Andrews thought that one was a meat-eating dinosaur, but he could not prove it. He did know for sure that one kind belonged to a plant-eating dinosaur called Protoceratops. Two of the eggs had been cracked before the babies hatched, and their bones were sticking out of the shells. The little skeletons showed that they were young Protoceratops.

Why hadn't they hatched? Dr. Andrews said that in this hot desert country, the sun usually kept eggs warm enough to hatch, after the mothers covered them with a layer of sand. But in this place there must have been windstorms, probably bad ones. Windblown sand piled up over the eggs. Some were crushed. Some got so little warmth that the babies couldn't live inside the shells. Finally, the bed of sand turned to rock, and there the fossil eggs stayed for 70 million years.

Protoceratops

9   The Cold-Blooded Mysteries

On August 2, 1841, a young British scientist stood for two and a half hours reading a report he had written. He and his listeners were paleontologists, experts in the study of fossils, and fossil bones were what the speaker, Robert Owen, was discussing. The bones belonged to a whole new group of very large and ancient land animals. Owen believed the creatures had looked like lizards. So he called them dinosaurs—or "terrible lizards." No one had ever heard the word dinosaur before.

At first, everyone mistakenly thought dinosaurs crept like lizards, low to the ground as in the picture above.

From the very start, people were fascinated with dinosaurs. Scientists themselves at that time did not have many answers to questions about the amazing creatures. They had not yet seen a complete dinosaur skeleton. They had seen lizards, though. At first they imagined that dinosaurs, like lizards, had sprawling legs and bellies that almost touched the ground. And so they believed that the bodies of dinosaurs must have worked in much the same way that lizards' bodies worked. For example, a lizard soaks up its body heat from sources outside itself—from the air around it or from a warm rock or the sun. When the weather cools off, so does the lizard. Its body loses heat. That is why lizards and other reptiles are said to be "cold-blooded." They have no way of controlling their own temperature.

When a lizard is cold, its heart slows down, and it can hardly move. In very cold weather, it crawls into a hole and waits for the air to warm up. If the cold spell lasts long, it goes into a very deep sleep. This is called hibernation.

A lizard doesn't have a large supply of energy when it is warm, either. It may hunt by sitting perfectly still, flipping out its long tongue at a passing fly. Or it may suddenly dart at an insect. But soon afterward, it will flop on its belly, all worn out. For every minute a lizard spends standing up, it spends nine minutes lying flat!

Were dinosaurs really like lizards? Were they cold-blooded and inactive much of the time? At first, scientists thought so.

Later, after many skeletons were found, it became clear that some dinosaurs must have marched nearly upright on strong hind legs. Standing on two legs means that most of an animal's body weight must be held up off the ground. Even when the body is not in motion, the leg and back muscles are not resting. They must be constantly at work, keeping the body's frame upright. So, a big dinosaur that walked mainly on its hind legs had to use a lot of energy, even when it was standing still.

Low-slung lizards do not have that kind of energy. To some scientists, it began to seem that dinosaurs were less and less like lizards.

The experts studied not only huge dinosaurs, but mini-dinosaurs. A group of small birdlike creatures called coelurosaurs was especially interesting. Coelurosaur means "lizard with hollows." These graceful creatures had delicate hollow bones, dainty heads, long curving necks, and very long legs.

One of the smallest coelurosaurs weighed only about two pounds. It was named Saltopus—that is, "leaping foot." Saltopus not only walked on its hind

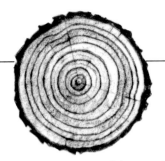

legs but could run fast, too. Its extra-long shinbones and foot bones were made for taking long, springy steps, and it ran lickety-split on the tips of its toes like an antelope or a horse. Can you picture a small, swan-necked body riding smoothly above feet racing so fast they seemed to blur? That is how Saltopus must have looked. Could it have kept up that swift pace for a long time? Scientists now believe that Saltopus and other coelurosaurs could, indeed, have done so. But if they were such swift, energetic creatures, they must have had bodies that were different from lizard bodies.

Not long ago a few scientists began to wonder about this. Was it possible that coelurosaurs were *not* cold-blooded like lizards? Could they have been more like swift-moving antelopes, which are called warm-blooded animals? An antelope doesn't have to warm up by lying in the sun. Its own body constantly turns food into warmth and energy. And it has a way of controlling its temperature, the way a thermostat turns the heat on and off in a house.

Suppose Saltopus had its own inside heating system. That would mean it was not just an overgrown lizard. And what about other dinosaurs? Suppose they, too, had been warm-blooded.

Scientists who liked this idea began searching for evidence that it might be correct. They took a new look at the bones of some big dinosaurs. Sure enough, the skeletons of duckbills and some others showed that they, too, must have been fast, energetic runners. This was one piece of evidence in favor of inside heating for big dinosaurs as well as for Saltopus.

Another clue came from duckbill dinosaur skeletons that were found far north in Canada. In that part of the world, days are very short in winter. The sun shines for only a few hours, and in some months there is no sun at all. Warm-blooded animals, such as polar bears, can live in cold, sunless country. Small cold-blooded creatures might find deep protected holes for winter sleep. But big cold-blooded animals could not stay warm enough with so little sun—or find big enough places for hibernating. This seemed to be a good argument for warm-blooded duckbills.

Scientists got still another clue when they studied how animal bones grow today in parts of the world that have hot summers and freezing winters. They found that the inside of cold-blooded animals' bones resembles wood from the pine trees that live in that same kind of climate. The trees grow quickly in summer, and a band of new wood is formed just under the bark. In winter, growth stops. Then it begins again the next summer, and another band of new wood is formed. Every year a new growth ring is added. Summer growth rings can be seen in cold-blooded animal bones, too. But the bones of warm-blooded animals have no such rings. What about dinosaur bones? Did they, like cold-blooded animals, show growth rings? They did not! Dinosaur bones resembled the bones of warm-blooded animals.

For these and other reasons, many scientists now believe that all dinosaurs were warm-blooded. Others say that some had inside heating and some did not. A few people still stick to the old idea that all dinosaurs were cold-blooded reptiles. Probably the experts will go on taking sides until more evidence for warm or cold blood can be found.

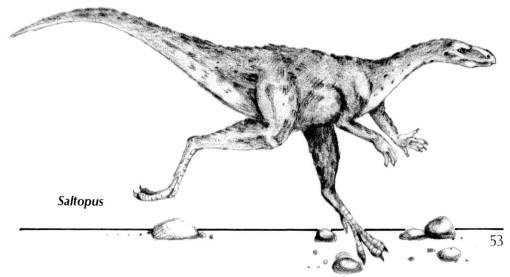

Saltopus

Archaeopteryx

10   Dinosaur Feathers?

More than a hundred years ago a man who was working in a stone quarry loosened a slab of rock that held a beautiful fossil animal about the size of a crow. The smooth limestone had preserved it so perfectly that the prints of its feathers could still be seen. There were small clawed fingers on its wings. And it had a long snaky tail—trimmed with feathers!

The strange animal was soon given a lovely name— Archaeopteryx, meaning "ancient wing." It certainly was the most ancient feathered creature ever discovered. It lived 140 million years ago. But was it a bird?

Archaeopteryx was not a bird like those we know today. It wasn't a flier, for it did not have the hollow bones that help make birds light enough to fly. Archaeopteryx's bones were solid. It did not have strong enough muscles for flight. And it could not have flapped its wings, anyway, because the arm bones did not join the shoulder bones in the right way for flapping. Some people think it used its wings for gliding down from trees. Others don't agree.

For a long time, scientists have thought that birds and dinosaurs were relatives. Recently, one scientist noticed something interesting. Without that astonishing crop of feathers, Archaeopteryx had a skeleton almost exactly like the small running dinosaurs called coelurosaurs. Was Archaeopteryx a feathered dinosaur? Why should a dinosaur have feathers? To some people the idea seemed downright silly.

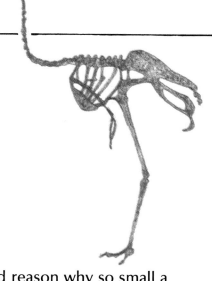

Actually, there is a very good reason why so small a creature might have needed feathers. Warmth! Big animals' bodies hold heat better than small ones, just as a big pot of stew stays warm longer than a small pot of stew. A big bare-skinned Brontosaurus could have lived through a short spell of cool weather comfortably. But a small, active animal would have found some sort of body covering useful. Feathers are both light and warm. They would have worked very well. So a small feathered relative of the coelurosaurs does make sense after all.

Was Archaeopteryx the ancestor of modern birds? Perhaps it was. But if not, then another creature very much like it must have been. Scientists have noticed, too, how much an ostrich skeleton resembles the skeleton of a dinosaur called Struthiomimus. Even though the dinosaurs are all gone, their feathered relatives are still here on earth today.

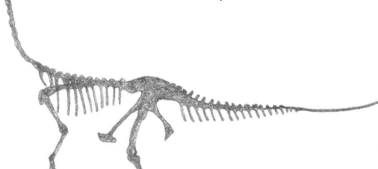

Struthiomimus

Pteranodon

11 The Hairy Devil Takes Off

The strange fossil creature had the bill of a stork lined with the teeth of a crocodile. Its hind legs and backbone were like a lizard's. The large-boned arms did not match the spindly legs. The hands were the most peculiar parts of all. Three fingers were upturned like the claws of a bat. A spidery fourth finger was as long as the rest of its whole body.

Some people believed that so strange a beast must have been a fiend or a demon from hell. Scientists finally agreed that it had been a flier. Its wings were sheets of skin stretched from the very long fourth fingers of its hands to its hind legs. So they named it Pterodactyl, which means "wing finger."

As time went on, many more fossils having wing-fingers were found. All were grouped together and called pterosauria, which means "wing lizards." Although they lived at the same time as Brontosaurus, they were not flying dinosaurs.

Pterosaurs came in many different sizes. One of the smallest, Rhamphorhynchus, was only about 18 inches long. At the end of its tail was a small blade of bone that might have helped to steady its flight, like the tail of a kite. One of the biggest pterosaurs was Pterono-don, meaning "toothless wing." From tip to tip its wings stretched more than 25 feet, though its body was no larger than a turkey's. Probably it spent almost all of its life in the air over the sea, diving into the water and snatching up fish. Perhaps once a year it returned to land to breed and nest. Pteronodon was a living glider. It must have soared for hours at a time, riding the air currents without so much as flapping a wing. How did it remain so easily aloft?

Pteronodon was built almost as light as air itself. Its wing bones, backbone, and hind legs were hollow tubes with walls as thin as a playing card. A system of air sacs, connected to the lungs, partly filled the hollow bones. The sacs worked like tiny bellows that were pumped by the moving wing. With air inside and out, Pteronodon could float like an inflated balloon.

Most scientists think Pteronodon could not flap its wings like a bird. It would have needed huge, heavy muscles to flap a wing twelve feet long. Probably the great weight of such muscles would have made it sink, and the straw-light bones would have snapped with the strain.

But if the wings did not flap, how could it have launched itself into the air? Because it was so light, Pteronodon probably could take off at very low speeds. It had only to face into a mild wind, stretch out its wings, and float up into the sky like a dry leaf.

For a long time, scientists have been puzzled about the long crest rising from the back of Pteronodon's skull. If the creature needed to be so light, why would it have carried a useless spur of bone on its head?

You can see how its long jaws stuck out in front like an immense pair of scissors. The crest balances the jaws. Without it, the bill would have made the head flop forward.

Unlike birds and airplanes, which steer with their tails, Pteronodon had no tail. So perhaps it used its head as a rudder to change direction, just as you steer with your head by turning it to one side or the other when you swim under water.

Were pterosaurs cold-blooded leathery-skinned lizards? Probably not. A life in the air would have wind-

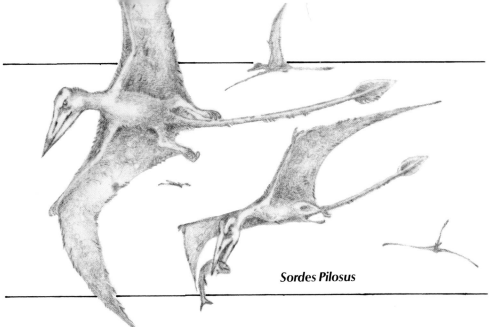

Sordes Pilosus

chilled a creature with bare skin. Then the pterosaur would have become sluggish and still, just as a lizard does when it is cold. To remain in flight, pterosaurs must have been warm-blooded. They also needed some way to keep warm. Then how did they prevent heat loss from their small bodies and huge, paper-thin wings?

In 1900, an English scientist said he believed that pterosaur bodies were covered with fur. Few people agreed, and he died soon after, not knowing whether he had been right. Then, in 1978, a Russian scientist found a pterosaur fossil clearly showing that the creature had a furry covering. He named it Sordes Pilosus, meaning "hairy devil." The Englishman would have been pleased.

The hairy devils must have cast shadows as they cruised over the open seas in search of fish to eat. Perhaps like those great fisherbirds, the gulls, the pterosaurs wore white. A coat of white fur would not be so noticeable to their prey, who would confuse their white masses with the clouds in the sky.

The biggest pterosaur ever discovered was even bigger than Pteronodon. From wing tip to wing tip it measured about 35 feet. People nicknamed it "Jumbo" and "747." Its proper name was Quetzlcoatlus. Quetzlcoatlus was what Aztec Indians called a feathered serpent that they believed existed in ancient times.

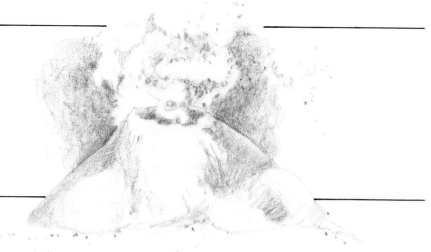

The Mysterious Disappearance   12

What happened to the dinosaurs? Why did the duck-bills and the great horned heads and the terrible teeth all disappear from the earth about 65 million years ago?

For a long time, this seemed to be a mystery without clues. So people tried to guess.

Some said the dinosaurs had been drowned in Noah's flood because there wasn't room for them in the Ark.

One person wondered if hordes of insects suddenly swarmed over the earth, the way grasshoppers and locusts do today. Could they have devoured so much leafy food that the dinosaurs starved?

Or maybe egg-eating animals gobbled up so many dinosaur eggs that finally none were left to hatch. At that time, rat-like animals did live almost everywhere. Perhaps they liked eggs, the way weasels do today.

There was one trouble with all these ideas. Dinosaurs were not the only animals that vanished at about the same time. Something killed big relatives of the dinosaurs that lived in the seas. Many kinds of fish and shellfish and certain tiny sea creatures died out, as well. So did many kinds of land animal, though not all of them. A very special disaster must have happened to the whole earth.

What sort of calamity could affect animals all around the world? Suppose the weather everywhere turned cold. Plants that needed a lot of warmth would die, and so would animals that fed on them in the water as well as on land. Plants and animals that could stand a cool climate would survive.

Some scientists think that the weather may have gotten too hot instead of too cold. Radiation from an exploding star might have started a heat wave. Perhaps cosmic rays killed some animals or kept them from having babies. Any creatures that could not stand heat or radiation would have disappeared from the land and from the sea.

Perhaps radiation or heat also upset some dinosaurs in a special way. Maybe they began to lay eggs that couldn't hatch. This sometimes happens to birds today. When they are upset, the shells of their eggs are too fragile. Many of them break in the nest.

Scientists have taken a new look at the many dinosaur eggs found in France. The oldest ones have thick shells. But the eggs laid nearer the time of the great disappearance have much thinner shells. Perhaps, at the last, no baby dinosaurs even hatched.

No one is sure how long it took to wipe out the creatures that had lived so well on earth for so many million years. Toward the end, the ceratopsians and some meat-eaters were the only kinds of dinosaur left. Perhaps some of them survived for quite a while. Or they all may have been gone in a few years—even a few months.

When it was all over, the earth must have been very quiet. There were no giant meat-eaters to roar at their prey, and no pounding feet when plant-eaters ran to escape the terrible teeth. Some large crocodiles still swam and bellowed at times in swamps here and there. Some kinds of bird nested and called in the trees. But on the dry land below, there were no creatures very much bigger or noisier than a cat.

Will we ever know what really happened? Scientists are always learning new things about the world. Perhaps they will solve this greatest dinosaur mystery some day.

INDEX